A FISTFUL
OF SKETCHES

A FISTFUL OF SKETCHES

Dave Hopwood

Second edition

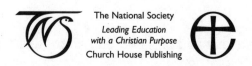

The National Society
*Leading Education
with a Christian Purpose*
Church House Publishing

National Society/Church House Publishing
Church House
Great Smith Street
London SW1P 3NZ

ISBN 0 7151 4969 5

First published in 1996 by The National Society and Church House Publishing.
Second impression 1999.

Second edition published 2001.

Cover design by 3t creative

Printed in England by Creative Print and Design Group, Ebbw Vale, Wales

Contents

Raps

Mimes (with music)

Prayers 'n' Poems

Introduction

I read recently that it is quite likely that Peter was a teenager when Jesus first asked him to be a disciple. If that is true then he must surely join a long line of famous biblical teenagers. As you probably know Mary is considered to have been in her teens when she conceived, David was just a lad when he smacked Goliath so effectively between the eyes, Joseph was barely out of shorts when he began to receive dreams and visions, and as for Gideon well … what can you say except he was the youngest member of his entire family. All this goes to prove one thing – youth must have its advantages. Of course it also has loud music, parties, homework, curfews, boredom, a million temptations and far too many hormones wildly out of control; but then you may count some of these as the advantages.

I had never considered that Jesus should choose a teenage following, but it makes perfect sense. Where else to find a group of people with the energy, the freshness, the nerve and the desire to break out and establish a new way of living.

Now, drama and teenagers do not always mix naturally, but the Bible is splattered with both. When it comes to drama Ezekiel is my personal favourite – you could perhaps think of him as the first mime artist. He did not have the most promising of starts. After being called to be a prophet God instantly told him that no one would listen to him, and as if to reinforce this fact God removed his voice. But there is method in this divine madness. If the congregation won't listen, then present your message in such a way that they won't need to listen – in other words – mime it. I recently went to the cinema. Behind us a gang of teenagers were draped in the corner, laughing and chatting their way through the adverts and trailers, which incidentally were aimed at the teen market. Only when the credits rolled and the hero emerged from the wings did they stop and take notice. They weren't interested in the talk and indoctrination of the marketing men, they wanted a good story with plenty of action. That's what the Bible is – a good, true, life-changing story with plenty of action. But the kids on the street may not realise this, so, like Jesus telling stories and demonstrating the new kingdom to Peter, we may well need to act it out in order for the teenage audience to stop and watch.

That's what this book is for – not to sit on the shelf, not for examining the theological implications of youth theatre through the ages, and it is certainly not a guide book for bringing adolescents into your church. It is quite simply a book to encourage the use of drama amongst teenagers, whether they are performing it, or watching it.

Setting the Scene

Small Beginnings

The first thing to say about setting up a drama group is that small is beautiful. That is not to say that a large group cannot work well together and present powerful and entertaining productions, but the bigger the group the more difficult it is to get everyone together for rehearsals. It is much better to start with a small group of three or four who can make the drama group their main church commitment, and so meet regularly to prepare. Many groups function by having a core group of three or four, then pulling in occasional members to fill out the cast. This works well all round, the group then have the freedom to do pieces with larger casts, and folks who can only do drama from time to time can drop in and out when necessary. This core group may consist of members of any age but this should be no problem. Drama is one of the best tools I know for bringing people together.

Calling The Shots

Having got your group together you will need to appoint a leader, as well as an artistic director. The two may be one and the same, especially in a group of two or three, but the roles do require different skills. The leader will need to keep the group functioning well, organizing rehearsals, cracking the whip from time to time, liaising with church leaders, making sure the group are happy about things, and organizing prayer times. The artistic director's role is on the creative side, such as looking for the right material and advising about props, costume, stage craft and performance skills. These roles are usually held by the person who has the vision to get the group started in the first place, but being gifted to do one does not necessarily mean being gifted to do both.

A Good Link Is Everything

Now begin to look at some scripts which are already around. If you can attend one or two drama workshops, go and see other groups in action. It is vital to watch the way other people work, to learn from their style and experience, and good to try out their tried and tested scripts whilst you are developing as a new group. Be cautious at first about learning pieces which are very specific. You may find a fantastic piece about Elijah and the prophets of Baal, only to discover after six months of rehearsal that your church did that bit of the Bible last year! Get together a small repertoire of pieces on a general theme. The love of God, the crucifixion, temptation, and prayer are all themes which can slot into the average sermon somewhere. I am convinced that a good link is everything! We regularly present an event at our church entitled 'On The Fringe'. It runs fortnightly and we don't have the time constantly to come up with new pieces, so I attempt to weave them together in different ways to fit a variety of themes. The great thing about a piece of drama is that one can see many different messages in the same piece. For example, *The Farmer* on page 13 could be used to demonstrate any of the following: the love of God, the rebellion of man, the good shepherd, the parables of Jesus, the way God searches for us, his reluctance to lose even one person, the fact that he never lets us go – no matter how sinful we may feel.

Dedication

Back to the group … Arrange to meet regularly. You may even need to carve out time, i.e. drop other commitments! I have no problem emphasizing this because drama is as important as any other ministry in the church. When it is performed well it can communicate in a way which nothing else can, and it's certainly one of the best ways we have of communicating with youngsters – inside or outside of the church.

Propping Things Up

You will notice from the pieces in this book that I tend to work with few props and no scenery. My training and experience has led me to use this style. A change of costume can be suggested by simply adding a hat or glasses, or a change of character by adjusting the body posture. I don't believe that many props are necessary as this simplifies the preparation and encourages your audience to use their imagination.

In a piece such as *Get Happy* on page 11 the actors must move swiftly from one scene to the next, changing character in an instant – to use props would slow down the momentum of the piece and make the action clumsy. Having said that, in *Honest Ron's* on page 32 I have included the use of a triangle which when rung suggests scene changes and pauses in the action; and I should emphasize that any of the pieces in this book are adaptable to include more or less props and costumes.

It is tempting to want to use a lot of props – but you really don't need to weigh yourselves down with vast hampers of clown costumes, rainbow braces, welly boots and waistcoats. Whether your group chooses to use many props or not, what is of prime importance is that they use them neatly and effectively.

On The Road

Once your group is together and meeting regularly you will need to find appropriate places to perform. This may already have been decided – indeed you may have formed the group to meet a particular need for drama in a service or event. Speaking personally, I have used drama in church services, school services, assemblies, classrooms, parks, high streets, pubs (though I don't recommend this really!), coffee shops, restaurants, theatres, on a barge (just the once!) and occasionally in the average front room. Wherever you are planning to present your material do bear the following in mind:

- visibility – sketches may need to be adjusted if your audience can not see below a certain height;

- audibility – if you are performing in a large venue it may be better to use mimes or pieces where only one or two narrators speak using microphones;

- performing space – wherever you have rehearsed, you can be sure that it will be a different shape and size to your stage area, so walk your pieces through in the new environment. When you perform, try to avoid going too close to your audience. It is uncomfortable for them and hinders your stage projection;

- sound equipment – if you are using your own p.a. try not to have it obviously visible. You don't want the audience watching you fumbling for the on/off buttons. If someone else is in charge of the sound make sure you brief them clearly beforehand;

- background noise – will you be competing with anything? If you are performing on the street try to use a pedestrian precinct rather than shouting down three double-decker buses and an articulated lorry;

- the nature of your audience – be careful to choose pieces which are the right style for those watching. If you are performing in church a slapstick piece may be completely inappropriate, whereas if you are going to a primary school an exert from *Richard* III may not really make their day;

- the nature of your pieces – if you only have a tiny space in your church you may have to edit any quick or excessive movement, if you are on a huge stage you will need pieces with a lot of life and colour, if you are on the street don't use dialogues or wordy sketches;

- arrival and preparation time (to adjust to your space) – don't turn up fifteen minutes before the event to discover that the band or music group have filled the stage with equipment and will be rehearsing right up to the start of the event. Allow time for setting up the stage, liaising with others involved and for organizing any sound equipment and backing tapes.

And Now For Something Completely Integrated

Performing in church presents a variety of problems. Will you be on the same level as the congregation (in which case they will only be able to see you from the chest up)? Are there any pillars? Are there choir stalls in the way? Is half the audience sitting behind or beside you? Will the person on the sound desk know when and how loud to play your backing tracks?

And still on the subject of drama in church, always try to treat your presentation as an integral part of the whole event. Try and avoid the 'and now for something completely different' mentality. You may be different in style to what has gone before, but you are not the light entertainment spot, or the commercial break before the spiritual bit. Your piece may well be humorous and should always be entertaining, but it has the potential to speak as powerfully as any preacher can. Remember that Jesus punctuated his dramatic stories with short sermons, not the other way round. Luke tells us that He would not say anything to them (the people) without using parables. So try and weave your drama into the sermon, or just before it, or to finish the sermon off – or even in place of it!

Also, be as creative as you can about how you use drama, and the very style of drama you present. A drama can be anything from a TV-style quiz show, a magic trick, a mime, a knock knock joke, a demonstration, a music hall routine … the possibilities are endless. And the venues also. Many groups go into prisons, schools and colleges; you might also perform in your youth club or CU, or use the odd sketch to provoke discussion in your after-church youth group or home meeting.

Action!

Once you feel you are ready to perform try to find a respected member of your fellowship who can cast a discerning eye over your presentation. Show your pieces and discuss them with her/him. Try to get someone who will say (gently) if the standard of performance is not yet good enough, and also whether your repertoire has enough entertainment value. In an ideal world your repertoire

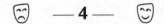

would be humorous, powerful, shocking, uplifting, tear-jerking and always leave your audience considering the message. Of course – it is not an ideal world! If only half my repertoire aspired to that! But with careful preparation, good feedback, innovative brainstorming, the courage to try something new, and a hefty handful of prayer, then most of the time your dramas should 'hit the spot' … as they say across the water.

And Finally

One final comment concerning drama and teenagers. Don't fall into the trap of thinking that a drama workshop is the ideal thing for your youth group. It won't be. No disrespect to them, but for many the teenage years are a period when dramatic and exuberant expression is embarrassing. They won't all be falling over themselves to practise stage projection or act out this week's Bible story. Some drama workshop games are useful and effective with your youth group as a whole, but only a section of your group will be happy about taking the show on the road and performing in front of others.

So, to sum up:

- Small is beautiful – and more easily manageable;

- Appoint a leader and/or artistic director;

- Fix a regular time to meet and make that an important commitment (whether it be weekly, fortnightly or monthly);

- Go and watch other groups performing;

- Attend drama and mime workshops and make notes afterwards;

- Get hold of some books of sketches and try walking through a few;

- Begin to put together a small repertoire on themes such as God's love, the cross, prayer;

- Present your repertoire to a respected person who is not a member of the group;

- Begin to perform as a group, always taking time for prayer beforehand and discussion afterwards.

Workshop Ideas

The following games and exercises are useful for encouraging and developing group skills and drama techniques. Many of these I have learnt and developed through attending workshops and watching others. You may like to adapt them for your own use, or create your own exercises which develop similar skills.

It is important to treat any group carefully and with flexibility; what works well for one group may be disastrous for another, and when working with teenagers they may be reluctant at first to try any of these exercises. From my experience I would say that girls are more willing than boys to throw themselves in, the boys may be very self-conscious and concerned about their credibility. However, most groups warm up as the session develops and by the end they may well have had a really good time. I usually begin with a fairly energetic exercise, and some games which help the group forget themselves a little, exercises which use a person's favourite subjects can be a good starting point. It is important to demonstrate each exercise beforehand so the group can see clearly how it should work. Try to have a good grasp of the exercises before leading the workshop – and try and avoid reading the exercises from the book as you go along!

Drama is really about play and unfortunately we lose this art as we grow older. Still, it can be exciting to rediscover this and that's what a lot of the following exercises are all about.

Famous Names

Get the group standing in circles of 6–10 people and ask everyone to think of a famous person, alive or dead, male or female, cartoon or real. Assure them that they will not have to impersonate this person, so they can choose whoever they like. Next, ask each person in the circle to call out their famous name as you progress round the circle, thus giving the group the chance to hear who each person has adopted. One person then stands in the middle of the circle (a volunteer!) and has to swap with another member of the group by running towards them and calling out their famous name. If they get the name right then the other person must run in and take their place in the centre of the circle. So the game is a memory exercise as much as a physical warm up. Each person retains the same name all the way through, and everyone must jog lightly on the spot throughout the entire exercise. When the group has got used to the exercise then increase the number of people in the middle of the circle to two, and then three.

Giving Orders

A good exercise for practising being the director, and being directed. In twos or threes ask each group to find a chair. One of the group must then lead the other(s) through a series of instructions, e.g. stand on the chair, turn around, smile, jump down, take a bow, clap your hands … The instructions may be as simple or as complex as you like, but the director must have total control and the others must follow the instructions.

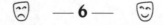

Birthday Line

A good one for beginning a mime session. Ask everyone to remain silent throughout this exercise, and then to place themselves in a line from one side of the room to the other, in order of their birthdays. Place a chair at either end – one representing January 1st, the other December 31st. Encourage the group by telling them that they don't have to worry about the year – only the day and month. They may not whisper, talk or mouth words to each other, but can communicate in any other fashion as they attempt to slot in at the right point along the line. When the line is complete walk down asking each person to call out the date of their birthday to see how they all fared.

Newspaper Bashing

A lively, somewhat violent exercise for the enthusiastic! In twos, sit and face each other, a rolled up newspaper lying on the floor between each couple. The workshop leader calls out a category, such as cars, or girls' names, or animals. As soon as this category is named either person may call out a member of that category then reach forward and grab the newspaper and begin bashing her or his opponent over the head with the paper until the opponent calls out a different member of that category. As soon as the opponent does call out, then the basher must drop the paper so that the opponent may begin bashing him or her over the head. No repeats are allowed so the longer the category continues the harder it becomes to think of new names to call out. After a while you may like to stop them all and change the category. The whole group may play this at once, or you might like to ask for volunteers to play this in front of everyone as it can be quite an entertaining spectator sport!

TV Channels

Divide into groups of 3–6 people and ask each group to prepare three television programmes, e.g. one for children, a film or a documentary, a news or sports programme. Give the groups five minutes to prepare these and then ask them to perform these in front of the others. Warn the groups that they must not prepare an ending for each programme, as you will keep switching channels. As each group shows their TV programmes keep changing the channels by calling out: 'Children's programme!' 'Film!' 'News!' 'Film!' 'News!' and so on, changing the channels rapidly so that the group has to keep switching from one piece to the next. This is a good exercise for encouraging folks to forget their inhibitions and to work together as a team.

One Word Story

A good exercise for helping stretch imaginations. Ask the group to sit down in circles of four people. Number each member of the circles 1, 2, 3 and 4. Now ask number 1 to begin telling a story – but only one word at a time. So number 1 contributes the first word, then number two puts in the second word. The story must then be told by the whole group, each person contributing just one word as you progress round the circle. The story must make grammatical sense. 'Once' 'There' 'Was' 'A' 'Man' 'Who' 'Wanted' and so on. Try this a few times, stopping the story from time to time and asking another member of the group to begin a new story.

Try doing this while the group is sitting with their eyes closed.

Try it whilst walking round the room together.

Try it lying on the floor, heads together, bodies making a star shape! The possibilities are end-less …

Now try telling a Bible story in this fashion, encouraging the group not to worry if details are missed out as the group tells the story.

Film Posters

Ask the group to get into fours, fives or sixes and explain that you would like them to now create a film poster, i.e. a still group photograph. Explain that most film posters are trying to give you some idea of the nature of the film, whilst also trying to make it look exciting and unmissable. So each small group must think of a film, or genre of film, and then create a dynamic, exciting poster to advertise it. When these are ready, ask each group to strike their pose and hold it while everyone else has a good look and discusses this. The effect can be quite striking. You may like to get the rest of the group to close their eyes whilst the presenting group moves into their pose, so that when everyone else opens their eyes they will see the finished poster without having seen the process of putting it together.

Now get each small group to create a film poster for one of the stories from the Bible. Explain that they can be contemporary versions of the stories. Again, look at each one and discuss.

Now form larger groups, about eight in each, and ask each of these to create a poster which weaves together several scenes from one story. For example, a poster about the prodigal son may have a couple disco dancing or drinking, alongside a character feeding pigs, alongside a person trudging home looking miserable, alongside two figures embracing. In this way we can see the entire story unfold in one picture. Some film posters use this style, weaving together several images from the one story. For your group it is one way of being a sermon illustration, holding this picture for several minutes whilst someone preaches about the prodigal son and the forgiving father.

Say Cheese!

This is a projection exercise. We tend to think of stage projection in terms of the voice, trying to speak loud enough for the audience sitting in the back row. But stage projection is also physical, and this exercise is all about the amount of energy we use when we act. Acting is a bit like being a Christian – it requires 100 per cent commitment. Often a performance is let down because the actors are embarrassed or lethargic about their acting. The way round this is to practise stage projection and to increase the amount of energy and commitment that your group puts into their presentation. Divide the group into two halves. Ask one group to take a seat down one end of the room. Now get the other half of the group to run from that same end down to the other end of the room, and on reaching the far wall to turn, call out 'Cheese!' and freeze as if posing for a wedding photo. Get them to do this a couple of times, demonstrating yourself how energetically you want them to do this. The more energy they put into their action, the bigger the picture will be. Energy is very attractive to an audience so the picture should become more entertaining as the exercise progresses. Give that half of the group a rest and get the other half of the group to have a go. Encourage the group as they begin to improve and increase their projection. They may well feel vulnerable and embarrassed, so they will need reassurance that they actually look good. Repeat the exercise, this time asking the group to run down the room, turn and say 'Wow!' as they imagine seeing something or someone which is amazing. Explain that part of acting is about reacting – i.e. that they must use their minds to imagine something amazing, which they then respond to in horror or excitement.

Now get them to run down the room, turn and yawn, again freezing in mid action. Explain to them that even a low energy activity such as yawning requires a lot of energy when you act it on stage. Remind the group that acting requires them to be someone other than themselves. Talk about contemporary film or TV actors and how they have acted in different ways.

Real Life

Divide the group into fours or fives and ask them to create a short realistic scene, rather like an excerpt from a soap opera. Give them the following topics to choose from: Homelessness, Church, Family life, Sex, Drugs.

Of course, you can offer them any choice of topics, but I suggest these as they seem to be current issues which are under debate and affect us all. Now ask them to create a short two minute scene about their chosen subject. Explain that they don't need to make a particular point, but that by simply presenting an issue in this way it will prompt discussion, and perhaps a practical response.

N.B. This is an exercise which you might use in your church youth group, but I would advise against using it on its own. Always try and use some other warm up exercises first to get your group thinking dramatically rather than going straight into these issues.

The groups must try to present these pieces clearly, with a definite beginning and end. Ask each group to freeze for two or three seconds at the end of their piece so that the rest of the group can see the piece is finished.

Parables

Jesus told parables all the time. They were effective short stories which had a wider spiritual and practical implication. In this exercise the group must attempt to create their own parable. There are two ways of doing this.

1. Take the story of the prodigal son, explain it to the group from memory, i.e. telling the story in your own words, then ask the group to split up into fours or fives and recreate that parable for some of their friends at school. If they keep in mind their target audience, it should dictate the kind of style and language they use.

2. Take the simple theme of Jesus taking our place and taking our punishment. Talk about the way he stepped in to help us, to set us free and to take our blame. If you have seen the film *The Bodyguard* you may like to use this as an example – Kevin Costner stepped in front of Whitney Houston to prevent her from being shot and killed. Again divide everyone into small groups and ask them to create a modern story that could present this theme of one person stepping in to rescue or save another person. Once each group has chosen their 'parable' they must either rehearse it and then show the others, or must pass their idea to the group next to them, so that every group is acting out an idea created by another group. This exercise is good in itself as it involves surrendering ideas to others and adapting to others' suggestions.

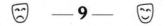

Teaching Pieces

It is good experience for the group to create their own pieces, and to comment on these, but it is unlikely that you will create a good piece of drama ready for performance in one workshop session.

However, you may like to teach your group one or two pieces from this book which they can quickly learn and present. Here are some suggestions:

> *Get Happy* on page 11
> *Johnny Cool* on page 50
> *Pentecost Rap* on page 52
> *Phil and the Gent* on page 55

These sketches are fairly easy to pick up as they don't require line learning, and they use some of the skills already developed in the previous exercises. I would allow half an hour to work through one piece, which should give you time to practise it a couple of times. Then, with one more extra rehearsal before you perform, your group may well be ready to present it in a service or youth meeting.

Get Happy

Bible Reference   The Beatitudes – Matthew 5.3-12

Themes   Happiness, quality of life, caring for others,
Jesus' teaching about our attitude to life.

Cast   Narrator
A group of four or more who respond to the narration
with the actions described in the brackets.

The group remain in a line throughout the sketch, the narrator stands at one end.

Narrator   You might well have heard:

(*All listen in different positions*)

That happiness is a McDonald's hamburger,

(*All open mouths and eat*)

Or a win on the lottery,

(*Look excited*)

Or maybe a fast car.

(*In groups, one drives the others look terrified*)

But think about this for a moment:

(*All think*)

What about the people who are hungry?

(*Hold out hands for food*)

And the ones who are poor?

(*Search pockets for money*)

Happiness does not come from what you own.

(*Hold out arms and shrug*)

On the other hand you may have heard:

(*Listen again*)

That happiness is a good joke,

(*All laugh loudly*)

A night out with the lads,

(Dance, drink, party)

Or a new wardrobe.

(Admire clothes in a mirror)

But I say: happy are those who don't ignore a problem,

(In twos, comfort one another)

And those who have the guts to go it alone,

(One stands away from the group, the group ridicules them)

And those who spend their energy on other people.

(Help one another in twos)

Money, sex and power,

(One counts money, whilst others drape themselves over and around him or her)

May well land on your doorstep.

(Open a door and look at the doormat in amazement)

But happiness does not come so easily,

(Still in twos, one whisper to another)

And satisfaction is a gift from God.

(All look amazed. All freeze)

The Farmer

Bible Reference	The lost sheep – Luke 15.3-7
Themes	God's love, his desire to come looking for us and to help us when we are in trouble.
Cast	Narrator Two or more actors

A group mime. The actors mime the same movements in time with each other, and in response to the narrative. Begin facing stage left, frozen and about to walk.

Narrator   I was out a-walking,
(Walk, stop and look at a signpost, then turn to face the front)
      Just the other day –
(Notice imaginary farmer, stage right)
      When I saw a man across the road, across the way.
(Freeze looking at him)

      He was looking down, well
(Become the farmer, look sad)
      He was looking bad.
(Look round for lost friend)
      He was looking like he'd
(Shake head sadly)
      Lost the only friend he had.

      He said he was the farmer,
(Hook right thumb under right braces strap)
      He said he was the boss.
(Hook left thumb under left strap)
      He said he was the best
(Mime holding a lamb and stroke it)
      Sheep farmer that there was.

      But he'd gone an' lost a lamb –
(Jump as the lamb disappears from your arms)
      It had run off in the heat,
(Watch it run, horrified)

And all that was left was the
(*Check shoes, peel off three lumps of droppings*)
Droppings in the street.

We headed out of town,
(*Open door, look in, stir stew with a ladle*)
Checked the restaurants too;
(*Raise the ladle, examine and smell it*)
And we looked for the joints
(*Grimace and shake head*)
Serving up the lamb stew.

We searched high an' low
(*Search around, behind doors, on shelves, etc.*)
Till the day was gettin' dark,
(*Narrow eyes, light match*)
And the wolves began to howl
(*Look, blow out match as it burns fingers*)
And the dogs began to bark.
(*Watch dog run past behind you*)
And it was gettin' scary
(*Back away, eyes wide*)
And it was gettin' weird –
(*Rub eyes*)
When the bright eyes shone
(*Watch rabbits jump*)
And the rabbits all appeared.

But he didn't give up
(*Take a rest, lean on fence*)
Not a chance, not a shot;
(*Wave a hand and start going again*)
He was looking for the lamb
(*Keep searching*)
Like the only thing he'd got.

And at last – what a shock!
(*Point frantically*)
Siree – what a fright
(*Break into a run*)
When we heard this bleatin'
(*Listen*)
Come a-beatin' through the night.

We found this lamb just
(*Push bushes apart, stoop down to look*)
A-quakin' in a rut,
(*Look up – rather moved*)
With his nose all bashed
(*Rub nose*)
And his ears all cut.
(*Hold ear*)
And the farmer he just
(*Reach down, scoop up lamb*)
Reached down from above
(*Hug the lamb*)
And he picked up the fella
(*Stroke the lamb*)
And he gave him a hug.

And his big old eyes
(*Wipe large tears away from eyes*)
They filled with tears:
(*Get so carried away wiping the tears that you drop the lamb!*)
He'd found his sheep
(*Realize, look shocked and scoop it up*)
And he'd lost his fears.

An' as I strode home
(*Back off, wave and turn*)
I thought about the lamb
(*Stop. Scratch forehead, stumped*)
An' I thought about the day
(*Scratch chin*)
An' I thought about the man.
(*Scratch back of head*)

An' I said to myself –
(*Remove hat, and ruffle hair*)
As I raised my hat:
(*Replace hat and mime holding the lamb*)
I hope somebody cares for me
(*Look up and clasp hands on your shoulders*)
Like that …
(*Shake head, turn and walk slowly away from audience. Freeze*)

The Ballad of Billy Fool

Bible References	1 John 3.1; Romans 8.38-39; 1 John 4.10
Themes	Self-acceptance, God's unconditional love.
Cast	2 narrators (1 and 2)
	A group who respond to the narration

The piece needs to be presented with vigour and energy, and delivers the basic message that whoever we are God loves us dearly.

(Group begin standing frozen, facing away from the audience in a line)

1   This is the story of young Billy Fool.
He isn't very clever, and he's not too cool.
He sleeps like a dog and he smells like a mule –
Should be in a zoo instead of going to school.

1   Picture a room – Billy's room. And Billy's in bed.

(Group turn towards the audience, hands above eyes, looking)

2   It's not too tidy, and it smells like something's dead.

(Group react to smell, saying: 'Ugh!')

1   Stale rubbish, stale food and stale underwear.

(Group mime holding up rubbish, food and underwear)

2   And the grease on the walls is from Billy's hair.

(Group run finger down a greasy wall)

1   But Billy sleeps peacefully through it all

(Group sleep and snore)

2   While his plants are all wilting from the smell in the hall.

(Faint in each other's arms)

1   Suddenly

(Group shout: 'BILLY!')

2   Picture – if you can – young Billy's mum:

1   A dainty creature at seven foot one.

(All cower, knees knocking, and trying to hide behind one another)

2   Fifteen stone with arms like trees

1   A mouth like Jaws, and reinforced knees.

2   But she had a real way with words.

(*Group holler: 'Get out of bed you lazy scum. Yer late!'*)

1   And of course, Billy obeyed immediately.

(*One of the group sleeps and snores. Others shout: 'BILLY!' They clip him round the head. He shouts: 'OW!' Others:'That's better, now off you go.'*)

2   Picture a classroom.

(*Group fight and shout*)

1   Picture a teacher.

(*One of group becomes a teacher: 'QUIET!'*)

2   And picture Billy too.

(*All sleep and snore*)

1   And picture Billy's mates … a friendly crew.

(*Look mean*)

2   They were a very close bunch, like brothers and sisters.

(*Assorted insults and comments:'Stop pulling my hair', 'You're sitting on my sandwiches', 'Who's that weird guy with the socks … Billy who?'*)

1   And when it came to a crisis – and it weren't no fun –

(*Mad panic. Jump into each other's arms*)

2   Billy could always rely on his friends –

(*All nod happily*)

2   To leave him, and run.

(*Group say: 'Bye!', wave and freeze, turning away from audience*)

1   So there lies the story of young Billy Fool –
         Looking very silly, and extremely uncool;
         With a mum like a wrestler and a brain like a mule.
         Life ain't much fun for young Billy Fool …

2   But hang on, that isn't the end of the story.

(*Group look shocked. Then during the following dialogue they look from 1 to 2*)

1   It isn't?

2   NO!

1   Why not?

2   Coz there is someone who likes Billy.

(*Group: 'WHAT!!!'*)

1   Someone likes Billy? With a heavyweight mum?
         But he's so uncool … and look what he's just done.

(*1 points at floor*)

(*Group: 'Ugh!! Leave it out, he's weird, just smell them socks. And with a face like that, he wants his head in a box.'*)

2   But there is someone who cares about him: God.

(*Group: 'GOD?'*)

2   Yep. He loves Billy, even if no one else does.
         You see – God don't mind how you cut your hair,
         Or the clothes that you got and the socks that you wear.
         If you don't feel cool, and your friends don't care.
         Just remember – God loves you and he's always there.

(*During the last four lines the group illustrate the words accordingly. Then all freeze*)

A Wild Time with Liz

Bible Reference	Jonah 1.1-3
Themes	An introduction to the story of Jonah; courage, purpose and obedience.
Cast	Narrator/God Jonah Girlfriend FX person (*Who creates the extra sound effects and dialogue over a microphone*) Team of 3–6 experts
Props	Stepladder, Megaphone (*optional*)

The narrator in this sketch represents God, who calls Jonah to do a job for him. Begin with the narrator, Jonah and his girlfriend all on stage. The narrator holds the megaphone and sits on top of the stepladder. Jonah stands with his back to the audience, chatting up his girlfriend.

Narrator   Hey! Jonah! Get off your butt and give us a hand!

FX   Kissing sound.

Narrator   I said: Jonah, get off your butt.

(Jonah shakes his head, not even bothering to turn)

FX   (*Negative*) 'Uh uh!'

(Narrator clicks his fingers, the girl suddenly steps away from Jonah, looks him up and down and scowls. She slaps him)

FX   Sound of a slap.

(She walks away. Jonah turns to face everyone, rubbing his face, horrified)

Narrator   S'better. Now listen. I got a wild job for you.

(Jonah looks terrified)

FX   'ME!!!'

Narrator   Yep.

FX   'No way.'

(*Jonah shakes his head*)

Narrator   Way, Jonah. Way.

(*Jonah looks at the Narrator, shrugs and shakes his head*)

FX   'Uh uh. I don't even believe in you.'

(*Narrator looks himself up and down, pinches himself and hits his face with his fist. The experts come on stage, inspect the narrator, measure him and pull him about. They nod*)

FX   'It's official. He's real.'

Narrator   Jonah, tell me something – who do you secretly fancy?

FX   'What?!'

(*Jonah looks horrified again*)

Narrator   Who? Come on.

(*Jonah looks at his feet embarrassed, he touches his face*)

FX   'Tsss!' Burning sound. 'Er, Liz Hurley…' Panting sound.

Narrator   Good! Now we're getting somewhere, 'cause I've asked Liz to help you.

FX   'Really?'

Narrator   Yeah. Now will you go?

FX   (*Lecherous*) 'Yeah' …

(*Jonah rubs his hands and heads off stage*)

Narrator   Oh, Jonah, one thing. Don't do this for her, do it for me …

FX   'Oh yeah, yeah, yeah, sure … '

(*Jonah nods wildly*)

Narrator   Good. 'Cause Liz ain't coming.

(*Jonah's mouth drops open, he looks crestfallen*)

        When I mentioned you she dropped out. But don't worry – I'll be around, so you'll do fine …

(*All exit*)

Jonah and the Big Man

Bible Reference	Jonah 1 – 4
Themes	The full story of Jonah. God's call and purpose for Jonah.
Cast	Two readers (1 and 2)

They stand on stage, left and right, and present this reading in a relaxed chatty style.

1 So here's the story so far.

2 Jonah's all at sea 'cause the big man told him to go to Nineveh.

1 Where?

2 Nineveh.

1 Nivea? Never heard of it. So instead Jonah goes to Tarshish.

2 Where?

1 Tar – shish.

2 That's a disease! Innit?

1 No it ain't, it's a stupid name. And Jonah went there.

2 To run away …

1 From the big man …

2 In a hurry …

1 On a boat.

2 You serious? You can fly to New York in a few hours and Jonah got on a boat?

1 Yep.

2 He has a serious problem.

1 Absolutely. 'Cause the big guy's waiting for him at the other end.

2 Does he beat the … (*Looks at the bottom of his shoe*) out of him?

1 No.

2 I would.

1 Oh yeah?

2   Yeah.

1   Yeah?

2   Yeah!

1   Well that would make a lot of sense wouldn't it? You pick a guy for an important job then just to make sure he does it all right, you break his legs.

2   I never mentioned his legs. That wouldn't be what I'd go bustin'.

1   There was a big fish.

2   What?

1   Shall we get back to the story here?

2   Oh, okay. There was a big fish and it swallowed Jonah. Which is humanly possible apparently. I mean, Jaws had three sequels didn't it.

1   It wasn't a shark.

2   No course not, but whales are similar.

1   Uh, uh. (*Shaking head*) It wasn't a whale either. The book says a big fish.

2   And you're telling me it swallowed Jonah.

1   No. WE are telling THEM it swallowed Jonah. It is possible.

2   Have you seen *Free Willy*?

1   Shut up. What happened next, then?

2   Vomit. It spewed him up on the beach at erm …

1   Nineveh.

2   That's the one. Bluh … (*Vomit sound*) Right on the beach. Bluh, all over your swimming trunks.

1   Bet Jonah felt cool.

2   Yeah! And I bet he found out who was boss, an' all. So he talked to the people and did the job like the big man told him too. Then voom.

1   What? Not back into the fish?

2   No! He went off under a tree for a rest.

1   Is that the end?

2   No. The tree died. Must have been the smell.

1   End of story?

2   End of story.

1   So er … what can we learn from all this?

2   Oh plenty.

1   Plenty?

2   Plenty.

1   Plenty. Like what?

2   I dunno, I'll have to think about it for a while …

(*Both freeze for a moment then exit*)

Wet Fish and Stomach Acid

Bible Reference	Jonah 1 – 4
Theme	A reading exploring the amazing story of Jonah and its relevance today.
Cast	Three readers (1, 2 and 3)

The three recite the Lord's Prayer together, as if in church, 1 and 2 interjecting as it progresses. The third reader remains in an attitude of prayer.

All   Our Father who art in heaven, Hallowed be thy name.

1   Er … just one question – how did you do that thing with Jonah?

2   Yeah, and why did you want him to go to Nineveh?

All   Thy kingdom come thy will be done,

1   I mean, what's wrong with London, or Milton Keynes, or Bognor?

2   And why do we have to have assemblies (*or church services, or appropriate event*)?

All   On earth as it is in heaven.

1   Can a whale really swallow a man?

2   That's bizarre isn't it? And why?

1   Why not just nuke Jonah if he's a wimp and get Moses to do it for you?

All   Give us today our daily bread,

1   Just how big is a whale's stomach?

2   And like, there's acid in it, isn't there? And gas?

1   He must have really stunk. How could he breathe?

All   And forgive us our sins,

1   I saw *The Abyss* where Ed Harris breathed fluid for 30 minutes –

2   But that was only a con, wasn't it?

1   Why didn't Jonah come out half-digested, with his legs all melted?

2   Why are these Bible stories so weird anyway?

1   It kind of makes it difficult to swallow.

All   As we forgive those who sin against us.

1   What exactly is a sin?

2   If I remember right Jonah went to this place to tell people to stop sinning.

1   Well, isn't it a bit out of date?

2   People don't do that anymore, do they?

All   Lead us not into temptation,

1   And what was Jonah's thing with the tree?

2   He went and got some shade under a tree and the tree died. Why?

All   But deliver us from evil.

1   This is well-difficult to understand.

2   Do you really want us to get something out of this Jonah thing?

1   Okay, you gave Jonah a job right, but it doesn't work like that now, does it?

2   I can't swim. I'm allergic to beaches. Whales hate me.

1   You don't still ask people to do things, do you?

2   Just in case you do – I've heard there's a lot of sinning in the Bahamas.

1   Yeah and we've got a week off next week.

1&2   Yeah!

(They say this enthusiastically, and for the first time 3 looks up at them. They flinch and shrug apologetically. 3 looks down again and continues praying)

All   For thine is the kingdom,

1   Where's Jonah now?

2   How did he get home?

1   Or is he stuck in a watery grave with some slimy, wet catfish?

All   The power and the glory,

1   Perhaps he should come back from the dead and tell us?

2   We'd believe someone who came back from the dead, wouldn't we?

1   Yeah. That's cool. That's impressive.

2   But then how could anyone ever prove it?

All   Forever and ever,

1   Has anyone ever come back from the dead?

All   Amen.

(All freeze, then exit)

The Adrian Puffin Show

Bible References	Joshua 5.1-9; 1 Kings 11.1-4; Judges 4.17-23 and many others!
Theme	A dialogue about the Bible and the many amazing stories it contains.
Cast	Adrian Puffin (Chat show host) Fergus Stump (His guest)
Props	2 chairs, cardboard box, large wooden tent peg, list, large Bible/book

The scene is a TV talk show – The Adrian Puffin show.

(Enter Adrian, a larger-than-life, rather smooth, confident talk show host)

Adrian   Welcome, welcome. Thank you. Welcome to my new programme, my little extravaganza if you like, my own little forage into the fridge of truth, my little delve into the dubious dinner of all things able to be delved into, my little excursion into the extremities of adventure, my little plumbing foray into the sewage of life. My show. The Adrian Puffin show. It's boring, it's old, it's gone, it's decrepit, it's forgotten, it's rotting, it's putrid, it's decomposing. What am I talking about, Adrian? Good question. I'll tell you. History. Open any history book and there it is. We can't get away from it. You can't get away from it. They can't either. History's here, it's now, it's happening, it's hip. Ask any decent pupil what they've got squeezed into their pocket tonight and for two five pound notes they'll tell you – a full-frontal, hardback edition of Strimpling's essays on the pre-disco period. Why Adrian? Why indeed. Let's ask the professionals. They're here tonight. No, I'm not talking about Bodie, Doyle and the other Scottish chap who couldn't run around so much. I'm talking about semi-professional, self-professed, unemployed, minor historian from Acton – Fergus Stump.

(Fergus enters. They shake hands and both take a seat on stage)

Adrian   Fergus, Fergus, lovely to have you on the show. First, I must ask you, the viewers would never forgive me if I didn't – Fergus Stump, sounds a lot like Forrest Gump. Is it embarrassing?

Fergus   *(Thrown for a moment)* Er … No Adrian, your name sounds remarkably similar to Alan Partridge, is that embarrassing?

Adrian   It's my show, I ask the questions. (*Turns and stares at him for a moment*) Fergus, history – is it just a shallow grave? Fill us in.

Fergus   Well, no Alan …

Adrian   Adrian.

Fergus   Adrian. Not at all. But it is boring. Believe me, I could waffle on for days …

Adrian   Yes, well, don't please – you only have five minutes, you're not famous you know. No one's ever heard of you. You're only on because David Attenborough's on holiday.

Fergus   Well, I'll move on quickly then. Let me show you what I mean. I have here some examples of the past.

Adrian   Ah, no doubt some rubble from the ruins of our redundant relics.

Fergus   Try this for size. (*He hands Adrian a cardboard box*)

Adrian   (*Inspecting the box*) Okay, let me guess, an old crumbling, fossil …

Fergus   Foreskins. Twenty thousand of them. From the crossing of the river Jordan.

Adrian   Ugh! (*He drops the box*)

Fergus   It's all right, they're all sealed in their own individual bags.

Adrian   What for – freshness?

Fergus   Hold this. Just an ancient rotting old tent peg. Archaic, slumber inducing.

Adrian   It (*Laughs*) it might even make you want to go to sleep!

Fergus   Quite. Belonged to a lady called Jael, she hammered it through an army officer's skull while he slept in her tent. Clean through his brain, mashed up his mind beautifully. (*Pulls out a list*) I have here something about King Solomon, heard of him? Right, well this is a list of King Solomon's …

Adrian   Mines?

Fergus   Lovers. Very virile. In fact, this list includes many boring aspects of life in the past, shall I …

Adrian   Oh please. Go on, Ferret, we could all do with an extra ten minutes sleep.

Fergus   Well, let me see, we've got orgies, parties, espionage, sex maniacs, babes, hunks, wimps, prostitution, carpentry, extracting money from fish, journalism, sheep farming, assassins, protest songs, time travel, achieving the impossible, war, how to get through 150 gallons of wine, gold, murder, bloodsports, learning a foreign language and returning from the dead. And these are all just incidents from one historical volume. (*Passes a book*)

Adrian   Fergus, thank you, history, it's all in the past now … (*He turns the book in his hands*) Hang on! From THIS!!! This book? All that? Amazing! Well, on that bombshell it simply remains for me to say – thank you to my guest, Fergus Gump. On next week's show I'll be talking to the woman who went up Mount Everest superglued to a rottweiler, and the man who drank 17 pints of guinness in two and a half seconds. See you then. Here's your Bible back. Incredible. All that's in there? (*They exit in deep discussion*) Amazing. He's in the Andes this week you know, David Attenborough, pole vaulting. Still, you weren't too bad … Not too embarrassing …

Silent Night

Biblical References	Matthew 2.1-12; Luke 2.4-20; Isaiah 9.6-7
Themes	Christmas, the importance of Jesus, the significance of his birth.
Cast	Director Three shepherds Two kings and two angels Mary and Joseph A sheep (*played by a girl*) A pig (*also played by a girl*)
Props	A doll for a baby, a pack of cards, a crib (*optional*)

The sketch begins with a group scene, all the cast posing around the parents and child.

Director And … take one.

(*They all talk and make animal noises at the same time*)

Director Wow, wow, cut, cut, cut. What's going on? Stop.

(*The noise continues*)

Director Shut up!

(*There is a sudden silence*)

Director Look we can't hear a thing, there's far too much racket. I think there's too much going on. Er … (*He looks down at one of the animals, played by a girl who looks up and scowls*) What are you doing, who are you?

Sheep (*Bored*) A sheep, sir.

Director Oh well, we don't need you. What about you?

Wise Men (*Both chewing gum*) We're wise men.

Sheep Who are you kiddin'?

Director Well, the wise men didn't turn up on the same night as the shepherds. They came much later on.

Wise Man 1 Probably went down the pub …

Director Look, go off in the wings for a while.

(*The wise men exit*)

Director Oh and take the sheep with you.

(*They come back and grab her by the ear*)

Sheep Ow!

☹ —26— ☺

Shepherd 1   Oi! Wait a minute! She's our sheep.

Director   Yes, but the shepherds probably didn't bring their sheep down, they'd have left one of their crew looking after them … Wait a minute … (He *prizes the shepherds apart*) What's going on here?

Shepherds   Playing poker, sir.

Director   Playing poker!

Shepherd 1   Realism, sir. We thought the shepherds would be the gambling type.

Director   Oh yeah, and I suppose you'll all be rolling a few fags next.

Shepherd 2   Eh, yeah, good idea, sir!

Director   Off! (*Points off stage*)

Shepherds   Ohh!

Director   The shepherds didn't stay for that long anyway. An angel told them about the stable, they came rushing down, saw the baby, then went back again, telling everybody on the way. They were too worked up to hang around for a quick game of snap. Go on.

Shepherd 2   Can we have our cards back?

Director   NO! Now who are you?

Angel 1   Angels, sir. (*Smile*) Flap flap.

Director   Flap flap?

Angel 2   That's our wings. (*Sniffs loudly*)

Director   There were no angels in the stable.

Angel 1   Yes there was, they were singing … it says so.

Director   Oh yes?

Angel   Yeah, 'Glory to God in the forest'.

Director   Highest. Not forest. The angels appeared to the shepherds in the field, not the stable. There was a star over the stable.

Angel 1   Oh we'll play her then.

Director   No you won't. We're not talking about Meryl Streep, a star in the sky. Goodbye. (He *looks down at another animal*) Who are you?

Pig   Pig, sir. Oink!

Director   They were Jews. There were no pigs. (*Points off*)

(*There is now only Mary and Joseph left, holding the baby*)

Director   Now that's better – no clutter. Just the baby, that's the important bit. Okay, action.

(*They sit silently, looking embarrassed. Mary coughs, Joseph clears his throat*)

Director   Well, say something.

Pig   What can we say, they didn't have an audience that night did they? Nobody else could have cared less.

Director   'Course they did. This was a turning point in history. There was loads of visitors, shepherds, wise men, angels … Oh, all right, bring 'em all back …

(*The entire cast come back on, talking, making animal noises. There is chaos*)

Director   So much for a silent night … Okay, okay, take a break … I'm sure it'll be all right on the night.

(*They all leave*)

The Wisdom of the Wise

Bible Reference	Matthew 2.1-12
Theme	Jesus came into the world as a lowly servant to those who would simply receive him.
Cast	Two wise men (1 and 2)
Props	A bag or case each, bottle of aftershave

Enter the two wise men. 1 is hastily searching through his bag, 2 is tired and rather irritable. They have been travelling for a long time …

1   You know, I'm sure I had it here somewhere.

2   What are you looking for now?

1   The compass! I'm sure I had it, honestly. I put it in when I packed the frankincense …

(They both stop and look at each other in horror)

2   Oh no, don't say you've forgotten the presents as well!

1   No, no, of course not… look – here's the incense. (*He pulls out a bottle. Opens it, smells it and reacts*) Whoops! No, that's my aftershave.

2   (*Desperately*) 12 months! 12 months we've been on the road.

1   11.

2   What?

1   It's 11 actually, 11 months and 30 days – see. (*Shows his watch*) It's only the 24th today, 25th tomorrow, then it'll be 12 months. You know, I think we might have taken a wrong turn somewhere. (*He stares into the distance*)

2   How can you take a wrong turn following a star?

1   True. At least we can rely on that star. (*Looks up, stage right*)

2   (*Looking up, stage left, so that they are looking in obviously different directions*) Thank goodness for that star.

1   You can say that again, can't go wrong there …

2   (*Suddenly realising*) Wait a minute, what are you doing? It's this one – isn't it?

1   Oh… yes, yes it must be.

2   (*Sighs*) Next time an ordnance survey map might come in handy.

1   Next time? There won't be a next time – this is an historic occasion – the King of Kings an' all that. Which reminds me, I had a dream last night.

2   (A *little cynical*) Another one?

1   Actually it was very funny. You'll never guess what happened.

2   Correct. I won't.

1   Oh come on, guess. You'll love it, it's hilarious.

2   Okay – you dreamt that it took us a whole two years to find the King.

1   Oh, be serious … Okay I'll tell you. I dreamt … (*Laughs*) I dreamt … You'll love this … I actually dreamt that a bunch of stupid shepherds found him before we did. (*Laughs again*)

2   (*Unimpressed*) That's not funny – it may be true.

1   Oh, don't be ridiculous. This is the King we're talking about. He wouldn't make himself available to any old riff raff, now would he? I mean – shepherds, they'd leave a nasty trail on his carpet. And how would they ever get in his palace? No, mate. It takes wise men to find him. Not simple folk.

2   Well, perhaps we should have brought a wise man with us then?

1   Very funny. Strange dream though – it all seemed to be in a stable. Ugh, yes, I remember now. A dirty old shed, it was. Isn't it funny how dreams can be so distorted. Must've been that camel's cheese.

2   Might be the truth.

1   WHAT! The King of Kings – born in a cattle shed – amongst all that … (*Grimaces*) muck! What kind of a king is that?

2   (*Thoughtfully*) Well, I'll admit an unusual one. But one who's not afraid to make himself available so that ordinary people can get the chance to meet him.

1   Ah, but if it's that simple, then why's it taken us twelve months to get this far? Lost behind this star? I mean, they call us wise men.

2   Maybe that's the problem. A king who comes to simple people can be a bit much for the wise to swallow … Come on. That star's on the move again, and I think we've got a long way to go yet …

(2 *goes to leave stage left*, 1 *goes to leave stage right*)

2   (*Looking back at* 1) This way.

1   So it is …

(*They exit*)

Persistent Widow

Biblical Reference	Luke 18.1-8
Theme	Prayer is often a difficult subject – to understand and to practise! This is a simple sketch based on the well-known parable where Jesus encourages us never to give up on prayer.
Cast	Jesus 1 2 *The widow and the judge are played by the same two characters who question Jesus at the beginning of the sketch.*
Props	Judge's wig, a copy of the *Financial Times*, knitting

Jesus is sat alone, motionless. 1 and 2 walk in already talking.

1 You ask him.

2 No, it was your idea.

1 Oh, all right … Lord, can you tell us about prayer?

2 Yes, Jesus, I don't understand it.

1 (*To 2*) Wait a minute – I thought you said this was my idea?

Jesus What is it that you don't understand?

2 Well, how's it work?

1 And why is it that sometimes we pray and we get the answer … and sometimes we pray and we don't? What's the secret?

Jesus There's no secret. Just keep on.

(*Jesus sits down, as if the conversation is over. 1 and 2 remain puzzled*)

2 Keep on? But for how long?

Jesus Forever. Don't stop. Always pray – and never give up.

1 But …

Jesus (*Standing again*) All right, let me show you. There was once a judge – a very corrupt judge. (*Jesus positions 1 as the judge. He gives him the wig*) He feared no one – certainly not God. (*The judge stands proud. He begins to read the* Financial Times) Okay?

(*2 nods, watching closely*)

Jesus And there was a widow (*Jesus positions 2 as the widow and hands her some knitting*), a very poor widow, defenceless and alone. (*The widow looks sad and downtrodden*) And one day she came to the judge, and said:

2   Hey you, judge. Yeah, you with the funny wig. I've been wronged by a man, and I want justice.

Jesus   The judge, however, ignored her.

(*The widow goes right up to him*)

2   Did you hear? I want JUSTICE! (*She shouts this. The judge jumps*)

1   Madam, go away.

Jesus   But she didn't, she kept on.

2   Justice.

1   No.

2   Yes.

1   NO!

2   (*Launches into a long speech*) But that's not fair, I've been wronged, wasn't my fault, how was I to know? What's the world coming to? I've been alone for 27 years now and one day this fella comes knocking on my door, I didn't know him from Adam did I? Mind you, he had more manners than you, young man, but of course, me being me …

1   Madam.

2   So I said, look at the price of bin liners, but would he listen? No. He was more interested in me dahlias, 'course if I'd have realized that when my late husband left them to me, I'd never have had 'em restored. Cost me £27 and that was before metrication day …

1   Madam, please! (*He is growing more and more distraught*)

2   But did he listen? No. Of course I blame the parents myself, always off to the wrestling, dinner in the oven, what's a poor boy to do? Well, I'll tell you …

1   That's enough!!

Jesus   And so she went on … and on … and on …

2   And if that wasn't bad enough he said I had woodworm. 'Woodworm,' says I. 'And who are you to say I've got woodworm?' So then I says, 'Now look here young man, you're just like your father, his eyebrows were too close together an' all.'

Jesus   Until –

1   MADAM! ALL RIGHT! I may not fear God or man, but you're driving me up the wall, woman. Yes, yes, whatever you want – YES!

2   So there's me – dahlia in one hand, bin liner in the other, woodworm under me arm …

1   (*Shouts in her ear*) YES!!! WHATEVER YOU WANT YOU CAN HAVE.

2   (*Looking at him with distaste*) Young man, there's no need to shout, I'm not deaf.

1   I don't care – I will be if you don't stop. You've worn me out. Whatever the request. It's yours.

2   (*Realising she's won*) Oh … thank you. And about time too!

(*They both freeze*)

Jesus   And if an evil judge like that will give justice because of this woman's perseverance, won't your Father in heaven – who is perfect – give you justice, if you keep on asking?

(*1 and 2 break their freeze and put down their props, to listen to Jesus*)

Jesus   And so my question to you is this: when I return, will I find that kind of faith at work in your lives?

(*All freeze*)

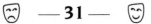

Honest Ron's

Bible References	Matthew 21.33-41; John 3.16
Themes	The parable of the workers in the vineyard. The Bible's offer of eternal life.
Cast	1 2
Props	Triangle, football rattle, large book, case

The scene is a market place. 1 and 2 enter and face audience. They narrate and act out the following piece. 1 produces and rings a triangle.

1 and 2   Greetings! Welcome to Honest Ron's market place! Home of fair trade 'n' fair play. Welcome!

(1 *and* 2 *separate and begin selling*)

1   Roll up – roll up! Every price knocked down!
Roll up – roll up! Cheapest buys around!
Roll up – roll …

2   (*Suddenly turning on* 1) 'ere! That hamster you sold me was a rat! You ever do that again an' I'll pull out your brain an' squeeze it up your nostrils …

1   Oh yeah! Well you sold me a plastic goldfish, and my cat got hold of it and was chewin' for days …

(*They are nose to nose and suddenly remember the audience. They turn, grin and 1 rings the triangle innocently*)

1 and 2   Greetings! Welcome to Honest Ron's market place! Home of fair trade 'n' fair play. Welcome!

1   (*Aside to* 2) Don't you go talkin' to me about rodents – your shop's so filthy even the rats wear rubber gloves.

2   Oh yeah! (*They raise fists and stand nose to nose. Freeze.* 1 *suddenly turns*)

    As you can see – business as usual! (*Exit* 2)

1   Now listen, one day just a few weeks back, this new geezer turns up – trying to sell some new stuff …

(1 *strolls stage left.* 2 *walks on stage right. He is whistling and carrying a case*)

2   Hello? I say – hello?

(1 *ignores him and mimes working*)

2   Er, I said – hello?

1   Roll up, roll up … thank you madam … of course they're fresh! No, that's supposed to be growing on there. Honest! (*Sells to imaginary woman*)

(*2 goes to a bag and pulls out a football rattle. 1 stops at the noise*)

2   Ah! Jolly good! Now listen you chaps – I've got this marvellous new product. Brand new. It'll totally revolutionize your lives and transform your market place. It'll impress the wife, sort out the dog, shut up the mother-in-law and settle the debts.

1   (*Impressed*) Hey! What is it?

2   THIS! (*He pulls out a large book and hands it to 1*)

1   A book! Forget it! (*He tosses the book and walks off. 2 hastily catches it*)

2   No, no, wait! Listen … (*Freeze*)

1   (*Rings triangle. To audience*) Well, I wanna tell you now how we gathered around this man, and listened for hours and hours in rapt attention, laughing and crying as he talked and we listened … But I can't!

(*1 shoves 2 who walks off disappointed*)

1   Get lost! Shove it! Push off! Go home! (*Pushes on each one*) Right! Back to work lads. Roll up – roll up! Every price knocked down! Roll up – roll up! Cheapest buys around!

             Roll up – roll … (*Freezes then rings the triangle again*)

1   Three days later … (*Freeze*)

(*2 re-enters*)

2   Er, excuse me …

1   (*Unfreezing*) Thank you madam – you won't regret it! Much …

2   I say – excuse me …

1   YOU!!

2   Yes, I've got this marvellous new product … aah!

(*1 beats 2 up. Use stage fighting and sound effects. Freeze*)

2   (*Turns to audience*) Now at this point you might be wondering just what's in this little book … Well … there was life – there was death – there was love and hate …

1   Truth and lies – now there's a debate!

(*1 and 2 begin to rap*)

1 and 2 Life and death and love and hate –
             Truth and lies – the big debate
             Power and colour and energy
             Progress and technology
             Biology, physiology
             Psychology with no apology
             Strong words, long words, bad words, good
             Backwards, forwards, ya know ya should
             A bird in the hand and two in the bush
             The battle and the hassle and the push-push-push

Life and hype and trouble and strife
News for a man and some for his wife
The good and the bad and the ugly too
The dirty dozen and the Scooby Doo
The Ten O'clock News and the Points of View
Top of the Pops and Radio 2
Back to the future and a blast from the past
The funky chicken and the monster mash
Talkin' pages tellin' the truth
Address the old and arrest the youth
Stop you – drop you – in your track
Follow the groove to the real love shack
Heavenly humour, deep direction
The way the life and the resurrection
Say – the way the life and the resurrection
The way the life and the resurrection … (*Repeat*)

(*This routine can become lively – leap frogging, dancing, clicking, etc. Abruptly the routine ends and they both freeze. Then 2 exits. 1 rings the triangle*)

1   (*Book in hand*) But of course – we never knew about any of this – 'cause we never read it. (He *throws the book away – 2 enters and catches it.* 1 *freezes*)

2   Er, I say, remember me?

1   (*Unfreezes*) YOU AGAIN! (1 *beats up 2 again*)

2   Now listen, I'd like to tell you about this volume of mine. Special offer. Absolutely free. No charge.

(2 *continues talking while* 1 *pushes him back and blindfolds him*)

2   Tell you everything you ever need to know. If you're frightened. Trapped. Sick. Confused. Lost. Anything you need to know at all.

(1 *stretches out his hands*)

2   It's all in here. This book will help you in any situation. In fact – I guarantee this book can give you … life!

(*At this point* 1 *stabs him with the stick from his triangle. Both freeze*)

1   (*Turns back to audience, cleans off stick and rings triangle.* 2 *is frozen behind him, arms stretched out*) So there you have it! Honest Ron's market place. Home of fair trade and fair play. Do call again. Good morning! (*Rings triangle. Big smile. Freeze*)

Bad Friday

Bible Reference	John 19
Themes	Good Friday, the suffering of Christ and his taking our place.
Cast	Two joggers (1 and 2)

The two joggers run on, wearing appropriate running clothes.

(They stop and collapse on each other, gasping for breath)

1   Whew! (*He coughs and gasps for a while*) There's nothing like being fit, is there?

2   Can't beat it. Makes you feel (*Coughs heavily*) great!

1   Never felt … better.

(They both gasp for breath)

1   Hey! D'you know what today is?

2   Give me a chance – I can't even remember my name at the moment … let me think. (*Suddenly downcast*) Oh yes, I know what today is all right.

1   What then?

2   My wedding anniversary – and I forgot!

1   No!

2   It is. I've got the bruises to prove it … just here …

1   It's Good Friday.

2   Oh no it isn't. Friday it maybe. Good – it is not!

1   It is – that's what it's called.

2   (*Suddenly breaks into another coughing fit*) I think I'm dying.

1   Funny you should say that – that's what it's all about.

2   What?

1   Listen, nearly two thousand years ago they took this man, put him on trial, beat him up, whipped him, stuck huge thorns in his head and then nailed him onto a cross.

2   (*Sarcastically*) Oh, I see. And that's why they called it Good Friday!

1   They thought they were doing the right thing at the time.

2   Don't tell me – he'd forgotten a wedding anniversary.

1   No, he was innocent. He'd never done anything wrong.

2   In that case he should have gone for a re-trial, like the Birmingham six, the Guildford four and S Club 7. Er, no hang on …

1   No, no – he allowed them to kill him.

2   Allowed them? Don't be ridiculous! You wouldn't do that. Not if you were innocent.

1   He did. On a cross, they stuck him up there in agony. And you thought jogging was bad!

2   Why would he do that, though?

1   Well, perhaps he took the place of someone else, someone who was guilty.

(1 *begins to jog again, leaving* 2 *thinking*)

2   Okay, yeah, maybe. But who? Who did he replace … (He *realizes that* 1 *has gone and shouts after him*) I said – who though? Who's place did he take on that cross? (T*here is no reply.* 2 *begins to run*) I said … (2 *exits*)

Careless Talk

Bible Reference	John 12.20-33
Themes	As the title suggests, talking glibly and carelessly, making promises and statements you can't keep or qualify. The cost of following Jesus.
Cast	Narrator Phil Andrew James John Peter

The five disciples stand in a line and pass their messages on in loud stage whispers. The narrator stands at one end and does not join in when they all speak together.

Narrator   One day some Greeks approached the disciples while they were in Jerusalem with Jesus. Together they asked:

All   Sir, we want to see Jesus.

Narrator   So the disciples passed the message along.

Phil   Some Greeks are seeking Jesus, pass it on.

Andrew   What?

Phil   Hurry up, pass it on!

Andrew   Some Sikhs are greeting Jesus.

James   Are you serious?

Andrew   That's what Phil reckons.

(Both look to Phil who nods encouragingly)

James   Pst, tell Jesus that some sheiks are eating cheeses.

John   Why?

James   'Cause Andrew said to tell him.

(They look at Andrew who smiles and nods)

John   Er … Peter, some sheep are bleating sneezes.

Peter   WHAT?

John   Shh! Quick, tell him.

Peter	Er, Jesus, I've got a message from John.
John	(*Points to James*) James.
James	(*Points to Andrew*) Andrew.
Andrew	(*Points to Phil*) Phil.
Peter	It's about shipping freezers, cheap – know what I mean?
Others	What?
Peter	Ships and freezers.
John	Sheep and sneezes.
James	Sheiks and cheeses.
Andrew	Sikhs and Jesus.
Phil	Greeks and seekers!
Others	Exactly! That's what I meant.
Narrator	And Jesus said:
All	Be careful what you say.
Narrator	If you're not sure what it is you're saying. And the crowd replied:
All	That's great. We want to follow you.
Narrator	Fine. Then do so – but first you must die. So be careful what you promise if you're not sure what you're saying.

(*All freeze*)

It Shouldn't Happen to a Vet

Bible Reference	Genesis 6 – 7
Themes	The story of Noah. The call to follow God.
Cast	Vet Noah
Props	Phone, papers, vet sign, mask, flippers and snorkel

The vet is seated at a desk with papers and a phone on it and a large sign reading 'vet'. Enter Noah. He is rather meek and mild, and quite nervous. Noah is wearing a swimming mask, and may also have flippers and snorkel.

Vet   Next please.

Noah   Good morning.

Vet   (*Looking up from his notes*) Good morning, can I help you? (*Looks round for an animal*)

Noah   Well, not exactly … but I might be able to do something for you.

Vet   (*Perplexed*) I'm sorry, I don't quite understand.

Noah   Oh dear, I haven't started very well, have I?

Vet   Well, you're obviously concerned about something. Is it your dog … cat … the ferret perhaps?

Noah   (*With a weak smile*) Yes, I mean, no, or rather … oh dear, I'm always getting my words muddled.

Vet   Ah! I see, you have the wrong room, the speech therapy clinic is two doors down. People do it all the time.

Noah   No, no – it's not me. No, I'm all right really. It's just that I'm not sure how to say this … (*Taking a deep breath*) Well, you see, my name's Noah and I'm afraid I've got some rather bad news for you.

Vet   For me?

Noah   Yes, I'm afraid so.

Vet   Don't tell me… (*Thinks*) A hamster with an ingrowing toenail – I admit that's a tricky one.

Noah	Oh no, nothing that bad!
Vet	No? Then your parrot's got tonsilitis? That's a difficult case. No? (*Noah shakes his head*) How about a sparrow with mumps? Your bat's going blind?
Noah	No you don't seem to understand, I don't actually have any pets … well, not yet anyway.
Vet	No pets? Then I don't see …
Noah	But by this time tomorrow I will have some … rather a lot in fact.
Vet	Oh I see, so you want me to come and check them over?
Noah	Yes, sort of. I'd prefer you to come on board with us actually.
Vet	On board? It's a boat?
Noah	Yes. Well, no … it's more of a ship really.
Vet	You're taking a pet on a ship?
Noah	Several actually.
Vet	Hmm … all right then, I suppose you'd better give me the details. (*Taking a sheet of paper*) Okay, how many?
Noah	Four thousand, five hundred and thirty six.
Vet	(*Writing this*) Four thousand, five hund … WHAT?
Noah	That's not including the fish of course.
Vet	The fish?
Noah	No, well, technically they're not animals are they? Though I have included the penguins in that figure.
Vet	You're taking a penguin on a ship?
Noah	Oh no. No, no, no.
Vet	Thank goodness for that.
Noah	I'm taking two.
Vet	You're out of your mind … I mean – you're having me on, surely. You're not really taking four thousand, five hundred and thirty six animals on one ship?
Noah	No. You're absolutely right, that isn't strictly true … really it's nine thousand and seventy two, well, we're taking two of everything you see. I knew you'd understand.
Vet	But all those animals … on one ship? You … you just can't.
Noah	Oh well, it's no big deal. I mean – it has got two floors, and the giraffes don't mind it on the roof.
Vet	Look, are you sure you're feeling okay? I happen to know a very good psychiatrist, and he's cheap.
Noah	Yes, I know. I've already seen him.
Vet	You have?
Noah	Oh yes, I've been round everyone in the neighbourhood. Well, I've got to tell them, haven't I?

Vet   Tell them what?

Noah   What the Lord told me. About the animals, and the Ark and all that water.

Vet   (*Cautiously*) What water?

Noah   Oh it's just going to rain for a month or two, that's all. Nothing to get excited about really. God's warned me about it, so I'd like you to come with us, on the boat. Otherwise you might get a bit wet. Bring your family as well, the invitation's open to all, bring the whole village, even your husband/wife if you want to. Only don't bring any pets, we've got rather enough as it is and we're only allowed two of each.

Vet   But I can't just up and leave the surgery.

Noah   (*Leaning close*) Well, between you and me you may not have a surgery pretty soon.

Vet   But the customers.

Noah   None of those either.

Vet   You're going to ruin me.

Noah   No, you won't be here either … unless you come on board of course.

Vet   But …

Noah   I'm afraid you'll have to hurry, (*Checking watch*) there's not much time.

Vet   What do you mean?

Noah   It's due to start raining in … seven minutes and thirty five seconds. Of course it'll be a few days before the tidal waves start, but the floods are due in the next couple of hours.

Vet   Rain … floods … tidal waves … But we're in the middle of summer.

Noah   Exactly. What else can you expect at this time of year, it's all a bit predictable really.

Vet   You're mad, you're absolutely crazy.

Noah   Mmm. (*Considers this*) Not really, although I can see your point.

Vet   Don't go away, I'm getting the police onto you, just don't move. (*Reaches for the phone*)

Noah   Oh, I wouldn't dream of leaving yet, we haven't got the greenfly on board, and I don't suppose you know where we could lay our hands on a female vulture? And you wouldn't believe the problems we're having with the caterpillars, we no sooner get them on board and they turn into … Yes, well, you don't want to know my problems. If only cold storage had been invented. Oh and if that's the police station you're after, I've already evacuated it.

Vet   Evacuated the police station?

Noah   Yes, I told them about the escaped sharks at the aquarium.

Vet   But there are no sharks at the aquarium.

Noah   No, but there will be in about five minutes, when the tide comes in. Well I suppose I'd better be getting along. Don't forget my invitation, bring everyone you can find, you're all welcome. (*Looking out of the window*) Oh dear, looks like rain …

(*Both freeze*)

Where Angels Fear to Tread

(Easter 1)

Bible Reference	John 20.1-18
Themes	The Resurrection of Jesus; his victory over death, hell and sin.
Cast	Angel 1
	Angel 2

The next four sketches follow one another, and deal with differing reactions to the Resurrection. Each sketch stands on its own, although the four were originally written to be presented together.

This first sketch is set in the garden, early Sunday morning, where two angels have an important task to complete. However, one is very inexperienced …

Angel 1   Shh. Do you wanna wake the guards up? Be careful.

Angel 2   Sorry. (*Sheepishly*) I'm not used to all this solid stuff.

Angel 1   It's called the material world.

Angel 2   Really? (*Trips again*)

Angel 1   Oh, for heaven's sake …

Angel 2   Isn't that why we're here?

Angel 1   Ha, ha. Now hurry up. We've only got two minutes to shake the gates of Hades.

Angel 2   Are the others bringing the fireworks?

Angel 1   What others?

Angel 2   Hey? You mean it's just us two? And no fireworks?

Angel 1   Nope.

Angel 2   Oh, well, that's brilliant, isn't it? How on earth are we gonna shake the gates of He … ahem … you know where, without any explosives?

Angel 1   All we have to do is move one stone.

Angel 2   One stone? But no one'll notice that. Can't we have some noise?

Angel 1   I think we've already had enough noise from you to raise the dead … which reminds me – we've got a job to do.

Angel 2   Where is this stone then? (*Wildly looking around*)

Angel 1   Well, where would you find the biggest rocks around here?

Angel 2   (*Thinks*) Stonehenge?

Angel 1   No. HIS tomb.

Angel 2   HIS tomb!!! You mean . . . (*Gawping at a huge, imaginary rock*) … His tomb? We're going to open that?

Angel 1   That's what Michael said.

Angel 2   But not … (*Looks up*) … that rock?

Angel 1   Yep.

Angel 2   (*Hastily turning round*) I'm going back for the explosives.

Angel 1   (*Grabbing his arm*) We don't need them. Just one push and it'll all be over.

Angel 2   What will?

Angel 1   Death and Hell and Sin.

Angel 2   (*Cringing*) Please! Do you have to use such bad language on a Sunday?

Angel 1   Sorry, but this is the greatest moment in history.

Angel 2   In that case we should have brought the singing group along, and had a knees-up like when he was born.

Angel 1   Oh no, we don't need that, just an open tomb, and an empty cross – that's enough for Easter.

Angel 2   Easter? What's that then?

(1 *looks back at 2 wearily. 2 shrugs. Both freeze*)

Rolling Stones

(Easter 2)

Bible Reference   Matthew 28.1-10

Cast   Officer
                       Jones

This sketch continues the series of Sunday morning events. While the angels prepare to shake the world, one very nervous soldier is on guard. He is smoking, then sees the Officer approach and hastily steps on the cigarette.

Officer   Morning, Jones.

Jones   Sir.

Officer   Got a cigarette?

(Jones raises his foot. Both stare at crushed dog end)

Officer   (*Awkwardly*) Ah … well … I'm giving up anyway.

(Pause. Jones looks around nervously)

Jones   Eerie, ain't it, Sir?

Officer   Mmm?

Jones   All this, the tomb an' everything. I mean, (*Laughs weakly*) I wouldn't fancy grave duty all year round.

Officer   I suppose it is a bit of a dead-end job.

Jones   There's a lot of rumours, Sir.

Officer   (*Considers this*) Very astute, Jones. There's also a lot of pork pies in Wiltshire, but I don't see what that's got to do with anything.

Jones   I mean about him, Sir. They say he's going to… (*Looks round then draws close to the Officer*) … reappear.

Officer   (*Deliberately looks round himself*) Well, if he does (*Beckons Jones closer*) he'll need a JCB to dig his way out of there. That tomb's got more rock than Blackpool.

Jones   It's no laughing matter, Sir. I don't like it.

Officer   Jones, you're not paid to like it. It's just rumours. The dead don't come back.

Jones   Tell that to Lazarus.

Officer   Jones, I don't want to hear it anymore. You're a soldier, not a five-year-old. What are you frightened of?

Jones   I saw him. I arrested him. There are things that I said and did that I'd rather forget.

Officer   We all gave him a hard time, that's the punishment for fanatics.

Jones   But if he ain't dead. If he moves that stone, and comes back to see me … I don't want him dragging those things up … I can't face that.

Officer   (*Abruptly*) Jones! You're relieved. Go and have a cup of coffee, lie down, watch TV. Anything to raise your spirits.

Jones   I don't want any spirits raised round here, thanks!

Officer   JONES!

(*There is a loud crash offstage. Both men stagger as the ground shakes*)

Jones   What was that? (*He peers cautiously offstage*)

Officer   Look, don't panic. I'm sure it was nothing.

Jones   Nothing? Sounds to me like someone's moved all that Blackpool rock, Sir … and I don't see any JCBs round here.

(*Freeze*)

Mary ...

(Easter 3)

Bible References	Matthew 28.11-15; John 20.11-18
Cast	Mary Officer

The scene is still the garden. The Officer from the previous sketch is now alone, jotting down notes from the scene of the 'robbery'. Enter Mary. She is running and out of breath. Without looking up the Officer stops her with his outstretched hand.

Officer   Excuse me, Madam.

Mary   Yes?

Officer   Would you mind telling me how you got in here. This is private property you know, there are penalties for breaking and entering.

Mary   I didn't break in, I only came for his body ...

Officer   Ahhh! So you took it did you?

Mary   I took it? (*Not understanding*)

Officer   (*Making notes*) Thank you. An honest confession is always the best way.

Mary   You don't understand. I've just seen him.

Officer   Oh, I understand the situation completely.

Mary   He's not dead.

Officer   (*Stops writing and looks Mary up and down*) Have you seen an optician lately?

Mary   (*Continuing with her story*) I thought he was the gardener, you see.

Officer   The optician?

Mary   No, no, don't you understand? I've seen Jesus. He's alive. He's risen from the dead.

Officer   (*Falters for a second*) There is a law against this, you know. What's your name?

Mary   Mary. Look, please let me go. I've got to tell the others.

Officer   Oh, there's more is there?

Mary   Yes, and they think he's dead too.

Officer   They're right. He is dead.

Mary No. You're wrong, I saw him. We talked. Oh, you don't have to believe me …

Officer Where is he then?

Mary Here.

Officer (*Looks around*) I don't see him.

Mary I've met him.

Officer That's no proof. That won't fool the undertaker, dear.

Mary No, but what about an empty tomb?

Officer Grave robbers. (*Losing patience*) Now show me where he is and I might believe you.

Mary I can't. He's here, believe me. Look around and you'll see. But believe me – he is alive.

(*Both freeze*)

The Road to Emmaus

(Easter 4)

Bible Reference   Luke 24.13-35

Cast   Cleopas
Luke

Enter the two disciples. Both are tired from walking.

Cleopas   Come on, we must make Emmaus before nine, it'll be dark soon.

Luke   We would have done it hours ago, if you hadn't got us thrown off the bus.

(The two stop to face each other)

Cleopas   I only mentioned Jesus.

Luke   Yes – but 27 times?

Cleopas   Just because he's dead, he won't be forgotten.

Luke   No. You made sure of that, didn't you? I mean, did you really have to offer the conductor a copy of *Journey into Life*?

Cleopas   Isn't that the kind of thing he would have done?

Luke   (*Glares*) Don't change the subject.

Cleopas   But listen …

Luke   (*Cutting in*) Don't you see, Jesus isn't popular right now. He didn't get that cross for bravery, you know. And we aren't exactly top of the popularity polls either, because of him.

Cleopas   You're beginning to sound like Pilate.

Luke   Oh … you're impossible.

Cleopas   I wish he was here.

Luke   Who – Pilate?

Cleopas   No – Jesus.

Luke   That's just wishful thinking.

Cleopas   Maybe, but what else can we hope for? What were the last three years all about? Why am I here with you now? Why don't I just go back to my old business?

Luke   (*Fed up*) I'm beginning to wonder.

Cleopas   You know, if he was here, he'd know what to do.

Luke   Really? I mean, what difference would it make? We'd still be wanted by the law, he'd still be hated by the church, my missus would still be mad at me for coming here with you on our wedding anniversary! Could he change all of that?

Cleopas   I don't know … I don't think he'd take those problems away, but then, he never was one for an easy life.

Luke   Shhh … keep your voice down … there's someone coming up behind us … and put that *Journey into Life* away …

(*Both freeze*)

Johnny Cool

by Chris Whitfield

Bible References	Matthew 11.28-30; Luke 19.10; Jeremiah 17.5-13; Psalm 1
Themes	Direction and purpose in life; the uncertainty of life; the need for God's help, care and guidance.
Cast	One or more narrators who deliver the rap Solo or group mime

A rap and mime raising questions about the purpose of life.

There are several options with this piece. It may be presented just vocally, with a couple of male characters delivering the verses along with a cynical, gum-chewing female chorus. Or you could add solo or group mime pictures to accompany the story. I have suggested one mime picture per verse, but you could add many more.

No props necessary, but costumes might be effective.

Narrator (Mime: *walking down the street, running hand through hair*)
I was cruisin' down the street just the other day,
Hangin' loose – no hassle, OK
My eyes kinda glazed had a real bad night,
Tryin' to look cool but my jeans are too tight.

(Mime: *face looks as if you are about to be sick, hand over mouth*)
My hair sorta shaggy, my breath a bit mean;
But my Hi-Tec boots are the hottest you seen.
My guts a bit shaky – had a curry last night –
But once I've had a coke I'll be feeling all right.

(Mime: *reaching in pocket for cash, while leering into a shop window*)
Cruisin' through the precinct – no place to crash,
Lookin' in the windows but I'm short on cash;
Checkin' out the action, movin' to the beat,
Wishin' I could slow down blisters on my feet.

(Mime: *finger rubbing left eye, shoulders hunched against the rain*)
Getting kinda boring … it's startin' to rain.
My girlfriend Nikki stood me up again.
Walkin' to the bus, water runnin' down my neck,
Hair gel in my eyes and my boots are gettin' wet.

Chorus (Mime: *eating popcorn staring wide eyed at a film in the cinema*)
Poor Johnny Cool tryin' not to care,
Actin' real smooth but he's goin' nowhere.
Poor Johnny Cool dreamin' big dreams –
Life's not as easy as the movies make it seem.

Narrator (Mime: *look of disgust as you sit shovelling beans into your mouth*)
Tea with my sister, beans on toast.
When will she learn I like spaghetti the most?
Didn't get a pudding the shops were shut,
Next time we're goin' to a Pizza Hut.

(Mime: *stare wide eyed as you press the remote control for the telly*)
Thursday night is bath night 'Wash behind yer ears!
Do like I say or it'll end in tears!'
'Turn it up Mum, give me a break,
I wanna watch the telly – it's time for Blind Date.'

(Mime: *press the doorbell at Dad's house*)
Come the weekend I visit my Dad,
He left when I was only three but I'm not sad.
He's splittin' with his girlfriend, Sharon is her name.
He said 'She had to go – she was being a pain.'

(Mime: *look horrified*)
Back to school on Monday yippy dippy dah,
Dave's had a prang in his Dad's new car.
He's comatose in hospital and broken his arm.
His girlfriend's dead though – she never had a chance …

Chorus (Mime: *light up a cigarette*)
Poor Johnny Cool – he's startin' to care.
He's beginnin' to see that he's goin' nowhere.
He guessed life was a game – nothing but a joke,
But now his guess is going up in smoke.

Part 2

Narrator (Mime: *walk down the street, arms crossed, looking worried*)
Cruisin' down the street, just another day.
Hangin' loose, don't hassle me OK?
My eyes are kinda glazed – had a real bad night.
I feel a bit shaky … hope I'll be all right.

Chorus (Mime: *empty pockets slowly, sadly throw away the contents one by one*)
Poor Johnny Cool he's startin' to care;
He's playin' a game where the rules aren't fair.
Life's gone and dealt him a real mixed hand,
Didn't seem to work out like he planned.

(Mime: *look around nervously, back away, bury face in hands*)
Where will you go Johnny? What will you do
To find something solid that's really true?
Where will you look Johnny, how will you know?
Who's gonna tell you which way to go?
Where will you look Johnny, how will you know?
Who's gonna tell you which way to go?

Pentecost Rap

Bible Reference	Acts 2
Themes	The day of Pentecost; the power and experience of the Holy Spirit.
Cast	Narrator Group of 4–8 who respond to the narrative

A sketch about the events of the day of Pentecost. Although it's titled as a 'Rap', it has no strict rhythm, only that which is kept by the narrator. The group who respond to the words should be between four and eight people; the action should be larger than life, and is described in italics beneath the appropriate words.

The group remain in a line throughout the sketch, the narrator stands at one end. To begin with, the narrator stands alone on one side of the stage or performing area.

Narrator Now not long ago down Jerusalem way
A bunch of folks from the town got together to pray.

(Group suddenly rush in, very excited)

Well, they prayed all night and they prayed all day

(They form a semi-circle facing the audience)

And they waited on the Lord to see what he would say.

(They mime praying enthusiastically, hands in the air, etc.)

Now they was all down, and they was all sad

(Wipe left eye. Wipe right eye)

Coz they'd just lost the best friend they'd ever had.

(Lean sadly, heads bowed, on each other's shoulder)

Coz the Son of God had just been around;

(Look up)

And he lived, and he died, and they stuck him in the ground.

(Look sadly at imaginary grave)

And for three long days he laid in that cave

(Some place flowers on grave)

Till the good Lord's power bust him out of the grave.

(Jump back in shock)

And when his friends all saw they were pretty shocked

(Jump into each other's arms)

Coz he walked through the wall when the doors were all locked!

(Look horrified)

But enough of the past, let's get back to the day

(Dust hands off)

When they all met together and began to pray.

(Continue praying enthusiastically)

And for a while nothing happened and they just got bored …

(Person on each end of the line yawn and wander off)

But they carried on praying and waiting on the Lord.

(They are dragged back forcibly)

Then all of a sudden – as a matter of fact

(Look up)

The Spirit came down and they all got zapped!

(All fall down)

And they all jumped up, started praising the Lord

(Jump up. Raise hands)

In languages they'd never even heard before.

(One person says a foreign phrase. Others look amazed)

Well! They had a praise meeting and the ground it shook!

(Some pray. Some read Bible. Some sing. Some praise)

It weren't like nothing in the new Prayer Book

(Throw book over left shoulder)

And Peter got up and he hit 'em fast

(One person becomes Peter and steps forward, others listen)

With a three point sermon like a shotgun blast.

(Peter punches his hand and holds up 3 fingers)

And the apostles translated every single phrase

(The whole group punch hands and hold up 3 fingers)

Into 9,327 different languages …

(They all look at the narrator in disbelief. He trails off)

And the folks couldn't cope when they heard it all

(*All look horrified*)

So they all came forward for an altar call.

(*Take one step forward*)

'You'd better be baptized,' they heard Peter say.

(*Peter wags his finger at audience*)

So 3,000 people took a bath that day.

(*All move and freeze as if diving into water*)

And once again the Holy Spirit came down

(*Look up*)

But it was all in good taste and theologically sound.

(*Look very refined, adjusting their ties*)

And there were healings and miracles, and wonders and signs

(*Pray for one another, or look in wonder at healed limbs*)

And the people of God enjoyed a mighty good time.

(*Smile. Shake hands*)

They prayed a lot together and they listened to God

(*Place hands together. Place hand to ear*)

And they loved all the people – even those that were odd.

(*Form a close knit group. Reach out to one person who is left out*)

And then came the message on the line from above

(*Form a line. One person answers a telephone. All listen*)

'It's time to go out and share the Father's love.'

(*Person on telephone mimes relaying this to the others*)

So they caught a bus, packed their NIVs,

(*Hands out for bus. Hold Bibles under their arms*)

And the world had it's very first missionaries.

(*Jump on bus. Hold hand rail*)

And the Church of the Lord – it's still the same today.

(*Face audience, point to ground emphatically*)

And we can all be living in the Pentecost way.

(*Some pray. Some sing. Some are healed, etc.*)

Coz we've been given God's power, and all of that stuff,

(*Each hold out right hand to audience, offering it*)

So that we can go out and share the Father's love.

(*Point to each other, turn and freeze walking offstage. All freeze*)

Phil and the Gent

Bible Reference	Acts 8.26-40
Themes	Philip and the Ethiopian; witnessing; the Holy Spirit's help and guidance.
Cast	Similar in style to the *Pentecost Rap*, this involves 2 narrators, who simply read alternate verses; and 4 to 8 people who respond to them.

Group begin by facing away from the audience, standing in a line and leaning on each other. The narrators stand either end of the line.

Narrator 1   Once upon a time there was a guy called Phil
(Turn smartly)

Who lived round the corner and just up the hill.
(Point over shoulders with thumbs. Look up stage left)

He worked very hard – coz it was his job
(All dig)

To look after the widows – give 'em all a few bob.
(Reach into pockets. Pull out money)

Narrator 2   Coz the guys at the top, called James, John and Pete
(Salute, stand to attention. 3 figures step forward)

Had better things to do than make ends meet.
(3 figures scratch heads, look dumb)

But Phil had the brains, and the 'A' levels too,
(All tap side of forehead. Lick finger and chalk up '1')

So he'd dish out the bread and the gladiator stew
(Some butter bread. Others ladle soup)

Narrator 1   Then one morn while Phil was on his way,
(Turn and step)

With his lunch and his calculator like any other day,
(Some bite a sandwich. Others use a calculator)

He turned round the corner and met a guy in white –
(Turn back to face audience, look surprised)

With wings and a halo and it gave him quite a fright!
(All pose as angels. Flap wings. Angelic smiles)

Narrator 2   Our Phil wasn't used to early morning shocks,
(Jump back in horror)

His hair stood on end and he dropped his sandwich box!
(One of group hold up hair. Others look at floor)

The Angel in white said: 'I've got a job for you.'
(Mouth these words, while pointing to audience)
Phil said: 'But I'm busy, and I think I'm catching flu!'
(Shake heads, back away, and sneeze)
The Angel said: 'It's Gaza – that's where you've got to go.'
(Point emphatically off stage)
'But there's a rail strike,' Phil replied, 'And we're miles from Heathrow.'
(Form a picket line. Look off into distance)

Narrator 1   The Angel wasn't bothered, he just took Phil away
(Shrug. Place right hand on throat, and pull)
And Phil landed in the desert, it just wasn't his day.
(Jump as if landing. Kick ground angrily)
Then came a carriage, with a really posh gent;
(Watch carriage zoom past. Look posh)
Phil thought he'd hitch a lift, so over he went.
(Hold out thumb)

Narrator 2   Now the guy in the bus was very well bred. *(Said with a posh accent)*
(Tighten up tie)
Went to public school, took his hols in the Med.
(Read books. Laze in sun, drink)
Had plenty of friends, and servants to match.
(Pat each other on back. All bow)
But with all his high living there seemed to be a catch.
(Look uncertain and shrug)

Narrator 1   Coz he still wasn't happy, and he weren't satisfied
(Look miserable and bored)
So he was reading the Bible, to see what was inside.
(Look surprised)
But though he pondered long, and he studied the Word,
(Group look deep in thought. Look down at book)
It weren't like nothing else he'd ever heard.
(Scratch head. Look perplexed)

Narrator 2   So just as the carriage pulled up by the side
(Pull on oversize handbrake)
He saw old Phil out thumbing for a ride;
(Stick out thumb)
So he asked him on board, he offered him a lift;
(Beckon with finger)
And when Phil saw the Bible he soon got the drift.
(Look deliberately; then tap side of nose, knowingly)

Narrator 1   'D'ya know what you're reading?' Asked our old Phil.
(Tap hand with finger)
'One doesn't,' said the gent, 'But one hopes one soon will.' *(Posh voice)*
(Stand in a royal stance; one hand behind back, the other out front)
'Sure,' said Phil 'I'm the man in the know.'
(Tap chest with thumb confidently)
'And while we have a chat can we go to Heathrow?'
(Point off stage)

Narrator 2   So Phil and the gent had a natter on the way
(In twos, turn and make mouths with hands as if nattering to each other)
            And Phil told him all about what Jesus had to say.
(One hand points upwards, other opens wide with shock)
            How he suffered and died, and hung on a tree;
(One person becomes Christ. Two others crucify. Others mourn)
            Then rose from the dead for everyone to see.
(Christ figure steps forward – ALIVE! Others are amazed)

Narrator 1   'What does one do now?' Asked the city gent.
(All assume Stan Laurel poses scratching the top of their head)
            So Phil told him to believe, and asked him to repent.
(Point to imaginary Bible. Bow head in repentance)
            And just at that mo. they were passing by some water;
(Point at water)
            So the gent got baptised coz he reckoned that he oughta.
(In twos, one pick up a bucket and tip over the other person)

Narrator 2   The gent was overjoyed, and forgot he was so posh,
(Look ecstatic, then realize and look embarrassed)
            Jumped in the river and had himself a wash.
(Step as if to dive into river)
            And when he came up with his sins all clean,
(Wipe face and stand upright)
            Our friend Phil was nowhere to be seen.
(Look round, shocked)

Narrator 1   Now if you're wondering what this story's all about
(Nod, puzzled)
            What we're trying to say is: 'Just Watch Out!'
(Mouth these words)
            Be ready for the Lord to take you where he will,
(Hands on throats)
            Even if you're busy, like our old mate Phil.
(All dig)

Narrator 2   Coz the Spirit's hard at work, just waiting for us all
(Stop digging. Look up. Dig twice as fast)
            To listen to his voice and follow up his call.
(Hand on ear. Watch something zoom past)
            No excuse will do, coz the Lord wants us in his work,
(Shake heads. Each point to themselves)
            And just like Phil – he can use any berk.
(Nod and point to person next to them)

Narrator 1   It isn't how good you are that helps him make his choice,
(Try and look good)
            It's the ones who are ready and will listen to his voice.
(Turn smartly. Hand on ear)
            So watch out for the angels, coz they're all working still.
(Flap wings, smile)
            And the Lord wants you to go – just like our mate Phil.
(Point to audience, look offstage)

The Bagman

Bible Reference	John 8.32. You will know the truth … and the truth will set you free.
Themes	Getting trapped, addiction, the power of God, freedom and hope.
Cast	The Bagman The Stranger A (*main character*) Four others
Props	Brown paper bag, black bin sack, four £5 notes, ten handkerchiefs

A mime set in a street or park, it may be accompanied by a song or music.

Enter the Bagman. He stands centre stage and looks cautiously around. He is wearing a long raincoat. Enter **A**, happily walking along, he/she passes in front of the Bagman, reaches the other side of the stage then stops and looks back. The Bagman smiles at them and nods. **A** shrugs, turns away and is about to leave when the Bagman stops them by miming whistling at them with two fingers in his mouth. **A** stops, goes back over to the Bagman and looks enquiringly at him. The Bagman beckons with his finger and **A** draws closer. The Bagman looks cautiously round, then produces a brown paper bag from inside his coat. He offers it to **A** who is curious and is about to take it when the Bagman snatches it away and holds out a flat hand for money. **A** sighs, shakes his head then pulls out two notes from his pocket and hands them over. The Bagman looks pleased and hands over the bag, then the Bagman saunters off.

A then carefully opens the bag and looks inside. **A** then looks up again and shrugs, starts to reach into the bag, then stops, looks round, and reaches in again. Very slowly, with finger and thumb, **A** pulls out a long coloured handkerchief from the bag. **A** holds it up and inspects it, then shrugs and throws it away and looks in the bag again. However, the scarf is still stuck to **A**'s hand. **A** stops and looks at it, then shakes hand in the air. It is still stuck. **A** waves it around. It still won't budge. **A** puts the bag down and tries pulling the scarf off with the other hand, it comes away. **A** is relieved and tries to drop it from the other hand. It won't budge. So **A** pulls it from one hand to the other, each time it comes off one hand and passes easily to the other, but **A** is never able to throw it away onto the floor. **A** then sees the bag and decides to use that, so **A** takes the scarf and shoves the hand and scarf inside the bag, then pulls on the bag, using it to lever off the scarf. **A** then removes the hand from the bag only to discover two handkerchiefs are now attached! [There are obviously two handkerchiefs in the bag at the beginning.] **A** is getting desperate now, throws the bag away and pulls one of the handkerchiefs into the other hand so that there is now a scarf attached to each hand. **A** walks up and down the stage trying to throw them away. This becomes quite vigorous and as athletic as your acting will allow!

Enter four others. **A** sees them and in an attempt to look cool shoves a hand in each pocket along with the handkerchiefs. **A** saunters around the stage pretending everything is fine. The other four walk around, all with at least one hand in their pockets. They all nod and smile at one another, then they move away from each other, look around and when they think no one is watching, and all at the same moment they remove their hands from their pockets and each is stuck to a handkerchief. They wave and shake their hands desperately trying to get rid of the things. Then they see each other, stop dead, look in horror at their own handkerchief and hastily shove their hands back into the safety of their pockets with a big 'I'm fine' kind of smile. Then they pull out their hands and repeat the shaking process again.

Enter the Bagman, grinning. They see him, rush over and gather round him, angrily shaking their fists and handkerchiefs. He stops them and calms them down. He rubs his fingers for more money. One of the group pulls out some. He snatches it and throws another brown bag at them, then leaves, laughing. They all scramble for the bag, it spills everywhere, it is just full of more handkerchiefs.

Enter the Stranger. He watches them as they angrily try to get rid of the handkerchiefs until they notice him. He is carrying a large black sack. He smiles and nods at them. He walks closer holding the sack and offering it to them. At first they pull back, so he walks up to **A** and holds it out. Cautiously **A** slips one hand inside it and feels around, it is empty, but when he removes his hand – the scarf is gone! He stares in amazement at his empty hand then hastily shoves the other hand into the sack and pulls that out minus the scarf. The other four see this then come rushing over, knocking the Stranger backwards in their rush to shove their hands in the sack. Then they all leave excited and relieved, leaving the Stranger to collect up any stray handkerchiefs and walk off with them in the sack.

Lean on Me

Bible References	Psalm 40.1-4; John 14.1; Mark 11.22-23
Themes	Our need for help, relying on others and trusting in God.
Cast	Traveller Stranger
Props	Suitcase, large coloured handkerchief

A mime to the song by Bill Withers, Lean on me. *It shows that there are situations where we need outside help. We cannot cope on our own, though we may not like to admit it.*

Enter the Traveller, he is carrying a rather heavy suitcase. He walks slowly, looking strained; as he reaches centre stage, the case feels so heavy that he staggers round in ever decreasing circles until he drops the case and has to take a rest. He stands facing the audience, gasping and panting. He produces a large coloured handkerchief which he uses to mop his brow. He sits on the case for a few seconds, then stands again and takes hold of the handle.

He lifts the case, pauses, then has to drop it again, it now feels so heavy. He looks amazed, pulls himself together and tries again. This time he manages to take one step before dropping the case. He takes out the handkerchief again, this time mops his brow, his cheeks and under his arms. Then he tries lifting it with both hands. No joy. He tries pushing it, then pulling it, each time straining like mad. He kicks it and falls over it. He gives up, sits on the case, looks sad and begins to sob heavily into the handkerchief.

Enter the Stranger. He takes a long look at the Traveller then slowly walks up to him and taps him on the shoulder. The Traveller jumps, looks up at him then puts on a big happy smile and nods as if he's perfectly okay. The Stranger offers to help with the case but the Traveller refuses, happily indicating that he's quite all right and can cope. The Stranger offers again, but the Traveller waves him goodbye.

The Stranger retires to a safe distance, the Traveller reaches down to pick up his case, then turns to check if the Stranger is still watching. Of course he is, so the Traveller smiles at him and nods, looks back at the case, takes the handle, then looks back again at the Stranger. He smiles again and forces a laugh, then looks back at the audience with panic written all over his face. He takes one last quick look back at the Stranger then takes firm hold of the case and lifts it. For a moment all looks fine, he takes one step, then collapses again. The Traveller laughs wildly as he waves at the Stranger as if he was only joking, then he turns back braces himself and is about to try again. He stops, thinks, shakes his head and gives up. Sullenly he steps away from the case, flippantly waving his hand at the Stranger and offering him the chance to try. The Traveller mumbles to himself as he waits for the Stranger to walk to the case.

The Stranger reaches down, takes the case in one hand and lifts it easily. He puts it down again, but makes no big deal of being able to lift it. The Traveller looks amazed and motions to him to do it again. The Stranger happily obliges and lifts the case again. The Traveller stares, drops his mouth open and begins to fall backwards in shock. The Stranger realizes, puts down the case and comes tearing round to catch the Traveller before he hits the floor. He wafts a hand in front of his face to bring him round.

The Traveller then reaches for the bag again, stops, thinks, then happily offers it to the Stranger. The Stranger lifts it, the Traveller looks around, decides which way he needs to go, then pats the Stranger on the shoulder and points out the way. They walk off together.

Don't Touch

Bible Reference	James 5.15-16
Themes	Temptation, sin, prayer, intercession, being set free.
Cast	Two, three or more people (1, 2, 3)
Props	Light plastic chair, a sign saying 'Don't Touch'

I have included general guidelines for performing this piece, it is fairly well known, though its origins are unclear! What I can say with complete certainty is – this piece is not mine! But I include it as it is a very useful storyline for street drama. The basic story is simple. A person sees a chair with a sign on it saying 'Don't Touch'. The person is intrigued by this, ignores the warning and gets stuck to the chair. They are then freed by someone else praying for them. There are many ways of presenting this, and many styles. It can be performed by two actors or more. This is often seen as a piece about sin – and some groups use a sign which has 'Sin' written on it. For myself, I think it is as much about the power of prayer and choose simply to use the words 'Don't Touch' and let the audience work it out for themselves. Most importantly – have fun with this piece, even when the person is praying; make their praying animated and interesting, they can smile and laugh while they talk to God. Enough waffle, on with the drama …

Enter **1**. He walks past the chair, stops, thinks, does a doubletake and returns to look at the sign. He reads it carefully, looks around then eventually decides to try and touch the chair. He almost jabs it with his finger but loses confidence and backs off again. He walks round the chair, comes at it from the other side and this time does touch it with one finger. He examines the tip of the finger, all seems well, so he picks up the sign, shakes his head and happily tosses it away. Now he flamboyantly swings his arm through the air and lands it firmly on the back of the chair. He leans on it, and shrugs as if to say, no problem. He then goes to walk away, takes two steps and stops as he realizes the chair has come with him.

He stops and looks back. His hand is still on the chair. He hastily puts the chair back and tries to shake it free. It is stuck to his hand. He lifts it with that hand and shakes it violently. No good. Without thinking he puts the other hand on the front edge of the seat of the chair and tries to pull the first hand free. The chair comes off the floor and he realizes both hands are stuck. He takes a long look at each hand and realizes the horrible truth. He leaps round, swings the chair through the air, throws himself violently around, but it is no good. So he puts the chair down and tentatively raises a foot to press it against the seat of the chair, he pauses, thinks about this then slowly puts his foot on the chair, as he pulls again his foot slips and he falls onto the chair so that he is sitting on it. He tries standing, now his bottom is stuck too. He shuts his eyes and shakes his head. Then he waddles around trying to pull the chair off; he hops along, but it is no good.

Enter **2**. **1** sees **2** and tries to look casual, **2** nods and smiles and walks on. **1** resumes waddling about; **2** looks back, sees him and wonders what on earth he's up to. **2** goes back and examines the problem. **2** then tries to pull **1** free, first by the arm, then by placing his foot between **1**'s legs and pulling on a leg, and lastly by placing an arm around **1**'s neck and trying to pull him off by the head. Nothing works and **1** looks shattered. **2** apologizes and shrugs. **2** leaves.

Enter **3**. **1** is now despairing. **3** walks up to him and examines the situation, thinks for a moment, then has a bright idea. **3** reassures **1**, then steps to one side, checks around to see if anyone is watching and places his hands together in an obvious praying position. **3** then begins to talk to God, obviously moving his lips, nodding, smiling, pointing at **1** and indicating his hands and backside. **1** takes one look at this and does not want to know. **1** resumes trying to pull himself free, but can't do it so takes a breather and leans on his hand. He jumps as he realizes the first hand has come free and he is now leaning on it! He has a change of heart and looks back at **3** who is still praying. He holds up his one hand in a praying position and copies **3**. His other hand flies off the back of the chair and slaps against his praying hand with a loud clap. **1** stares wide eyed and now really gets into praying, so much so that he wears himself out. He pauses for a moment and stands to stretch and scratch his back. He jumps as he realizes he is free, then rushes over to **3**, shakes him excitedly to let him know and they both look amazed and happy. Before leaving they both tentatively slip the sign back on the chair …

The First Day of Christmas

Bible References   Matthew 2.1-12; Luke 2.4-20; Isaiah 9.6-7

Themes   The ingredients of the first Christmas. Jesus was
                         born to set us free.

Cast   One Reader

On the first day of Christmas all this was sent to me:
Twelve hours of travelling,
Eleven refusals of shelter,
Ten smelly stables,
Nine months pregnant.
Eight hours of labour –
Seven animals watching,
A six o'clock birth
Five minutes' peace.
Four shepherds,
Three wise men,
Two startled doves,
And a baby to set the world free.

Paradise

Bible References	Psalm 16.11; Jeremiah 29.11; Proverbs 3.6
Theme	A prayer about the future.
Cast	One Reader

Dear God,
There are plenty of things I aim to do,
And many secret fears I have about the future.
Help me to think as big as you want me to,
To imagine heaven as it really is and to aim for it.
You know what success feels like
And you know about failure.
You know what it's like to be let down
And you know what it's like to win.
Help me make a success of my life
Even if it's difficult.
Help me to become the person
You planned me to be.
Help me when I feel discouraged about the future
Help me when I am afraid of death,
And help me to discover the true meaning of paradise.
I ask you this in the name of the one who experienced true life
And offers it to us.
Amen.

Unless

Bible References   Matthew 19.13-15; 1 Timothy 4.11-16;
                         Mark 10.13-15

Themes   The qualities of being young; a reminder that
                         God wants to use teenagers.

Cast   One Reader

Unless you become like a teenager
It is very difficult to enter the kingdom of heaven.
Without possessing dreams,
Without going against the grain,
Without a taste for rebellion,
And a craving for something better,
There is little hope of ever leaving this world to enter the next.

So don't let your dreams be crushed.
Don't be conformed to the world around you.
Rebel against the mediocre, the bland and the lukewarm
And always set your hopes high.
Then, with the currency of justice, mercy and humility
You will walk with your head high into a brave new world.
And nothing will stop you.

Also available:

Same author. Same style. Different content.
If you liked one, you'll like the other.
Simple really.

For a full list of our drama titles call 020 7898 1451

Price: £7.95   ISBN: 0 7151 49709
Available from all good Christian bookshops or call 020 7898 1300.

Doing drama too much of a palaver?
Not any more.

Designed to build up your confidence in using drama with children

❖

User-friendly scripts

❖

Good introduction to drama techniques

❖

Creative use of biblical and historical characters

❖

Ideal to use for collective worship or during an all-age service

❖

All the material is fully photocopiable for use within your church,
school or youth group

❖ ❖ ❖ ❖ ❖ ❖

The Good Rollerblader and other sketches
£7.95   07151 4944 X

❖ ❖ ❖ ❖ ❖ ❖

The Rich Pop Star and other sketches
£7.95   0 7151 4956 3

"A very practical and
humorous introduction to the art
of performance for everyone
involved with children."

**Peter Ball, Headteacher, Bulwell St Mary's Church
of England Primary and Nursery School, Nottingham.**

The National Society
*Leading Education
with a Christian Purpose*
Church House Publishing